Jason Kidd

Leader on the Court

Titles in the **SPORTS LEADERS** *Series:*

Vince Carter
0-7660-2173-4

Allen Iverson
0-7660-2174-2

Derek Jeter
0-7660-2035-5

Jason Kidd
0-7660-2214-5

Shaquille O'Neal
0-7660-2175-0

Jason Kidd

Leader on the Court

Ken Rappoport

Enslow Publishers, Inc.

40 Industrial Road	PO Box 38
Box 398	Aldershot
Berkeley Heights, NJ 07922	Hants GU12 6BP
USA	UK

http://www.enslow.com

Library of Congress Cataloging-in-Publication Data

Rappoport, Ken.
    Jason Kidd : leader on the court / Ken Rappoport.
       v. cm. — (Sports leaders)
    Includes bibliographical references and index.
    Contents: A most amazing game — Golden boy — A golden bear — The next
level — All-star Kidd — Bumpy season, breakout game — Golden — Jason to
the rescue.
    ISBN 0-7660-2214-5
    1. Kidd, Jason—Juvenile literature. 2. Basketball players—United States—
Biography—Juvenile literature. [1. Kidd, Jason. 2. Basketball players. 3. Racially
mixed people—Biography.] I. Title. II. Sports leaders series.
GV884.K53R36 2004
796.323'092—dc22

                    2003027973

Printed in the United States of America

10 9 8 7 6 5 4 3 2 1

To Our Readers:
We have done our best to make sure all Internet Addresses in this book were active and
appropriate when we went to press. However, the author and the publisher have no control over and assume no liability for the material available on those Internet sites or on
other Web sites they may link to. Any comments or suggestions can be sent by e-mail to
comments@enslow.com or to the address on the back cover.

CONTENTS

A MOST AMAZING GAME

Jason Kidd was angry. How could his team, the New Jersey Nets, play so poorly in the 2002 NBA playoffs? And now they had only one chance to save the season. It was win or go home.

The Nets were getting ready to play the Indiana Pacers in the fifth and final game of their first-round series. Kidd stopped a film session. He lashed out at his teammates.

"We all looked around and knew what needed to be done," said Richard Jefferson. "He's our leader, and we have to follow him."[1]

But actually doing it was something else. The Nets were coming off one of their worst performances of the season. They had been embarrassed by the Pacers in Game 4, losing by 23 points. More importantly, they had allowed the Pacers to tie the series at two games apiece.

The loss was unusual for the Nets, who had just finished a remarkable season. Kidd had been the main reason. After acquiring Kidd in a trade with Phoenix in 2001, the Nets went from a last-place team to tops in their conference—an improvement of 26 games! With a 52–30 record, the Nets had completed the greatest regular season in franchise history.

Along the way, Kidd was picked for the All-NBA first team and named to the All-Defensive team. The honors were, for the moment, secondary to Kidd, however. "Right now, I've got something bigger on my plate – winning Game 5," he said.[2]

Although the Nets were ranked number one and Indiana number eight in the Eastern Conference playoffs, the Pacers had been a tough foe to handle. They had won the opener of the series in New Jersey. And after the Nets won two straight to take a 2–1 lead, Indiana roared back for a surprisingly easy 97–74 victory in Game 4. Now the whole season was at stake for the Nets, not to mention Kidd's reputation. "We've had a great season," he said, "but we don't want it to end yet."[3]

With the roar of a sellout crowd of 20,049 at the Continental Airlines Arena ringing in their ears, the Nets looked motivated. They jumped out to a 19–9 lead. But the Pacers rallied and the teams went into the dressing room at halftime tied at 51.

By the end of the third quarter it was 79–79 and still anybody's game late in the fourth. The Nets suddenly reeled off 10 points to take a 90–81 lead with a little more than five minutes remaining. Game over? Not by a long shot. Or, more specifically, Reggie Miller's long shot. The Indiana star, who had been relatively quiet, fired in a three-pointer to cut the Nets' lead to 90–86 with about four minutes left.

> "We've had a great season, but we don't want it to end yet."
> —Jason Kidd

Miller was one of the best long-range shooters in the NBA, with a history of dramatic last-second, game-saving shots. If he were to suddenly get hot, the Nets would be in trouble. With 19 seconds left, the Nets held a 94–91 lead that was anything but safe. The final 19 seconds of regulation can seem like an eternity in the NBA. And this time was no different.

Miller, guarded by Keith Van Horn, had the ball thirty feet from the basket—three-point territory, but a stretch for even the All-Star guard. He faked a shot. Van Horn went up with Miller—and then came

Nets point guard Jason Kidd guards the Pacers' Reggie Miller in the deciding fifth game of the first-round playoff series between New Jersey and Indiana on May 2, 2002.

down on him! The referee whistled a foul on Van Horn. Miller was going to the free throw line for three shots. "My big thing is trying not to give up a three," said Van Horn, angry at himself for fouling Miller. "He's so good at drawing that foul. He's probably one of the best in league history."[4] Miller walked to the foul line. Van Horn, one of the Nets' key starters, walked to the bench. He had fouled out of the game.

Miller made the first shot. After a Nets timeout, he missed the second. Then he made the third. The Nets still clung to a 94–93 lead.

Now it was Kidd's turn. He made two free throws to give the Nets a three-point lead again. Later, when Jefferson was fouled going up for a rebound, he was awarded two free throws. The Nets appeared to be home free. There were just five seconds left in regulation. All Jefferson had to do was make one of two free throws and New Jersey would be victorious.

No such luck. He missed both and the door was still open for Indiana. And Miller took advantage, hitting an off-balance 35-footer in Kidd's face as time ran out. Game tied, 96–96! But not without controversy. The Nets claimed that Miller's shot did not beat the buzzer. TV replays seemed to support the

Jason Kidd beats Indiana point guard Jamaal Tinsley to a rebound.

Nets. No matter, the game was going into overtime and the Nets were wondering what they had to do to win the game. They had been leading by nine points with five minutes to go, then by three with five seconds left and the ball in their hands at the foul line. "I knew the better team was going to prevail," Jefferson said, meaning the Nets, of course.[5]

In overtime, it looked like the Pacers were the better team. With 1:30 left, Miller sank a three-pointer to give Indiana a 103–100 lead.

But, hold on. Kidd scored on a jump shot from 19 feet. Then, driving toward the basket, he flipped in an off-balance shot. Shortly thereafter, he found Kenyon Martin open for an easy dunk shot. With 26 seconds remaining, the Nets had reclaimed the lead, 106–105.

"When they needed a basket, he gave it to them," Miller said of Kidd. "That's why he's the MVP."[6]

Miller was pretty good himself. After the Nets inched ahead 107–105 with a free throw, the Pacers' guard threw down a two-handed dunk to tie the score.

Kidd's last-second attempt at the buzzer bounced off the rim. Time for a second overtime. The Battle of the All-Star guards—Kidd vs. Miller—would continue for at least five more minutes. "These guys didn't

Kidd drives past Jamaal Tinsley on his way to the hoop.

want to go home yet," Head Coach Byron Scott said of his Nets.[7]

In the second OT, it was Kidd in command. While Miller was missing all four of his shots and Jason Kidd's teammates were missing most of theirs, Kidd was making his count. Each of them was a dagger in the Pacers' hearts. With 3:06 left, Kidd's 17-foot jumper gave the Nets a 112–107 lead. Then, with 1:09 remaining, his 21-footer made it 114–109. The last shot sealed it as the Nets pulled away to a 120–109 victory in one of the most exciting playoff games in NBA history.

Talk about a pressure performance! From the start of the second half through the two overtimes, Kidd had scored 24 points. His 31 overall matched Miller's total. While playing 51 minutes, the Nets' guard added 8 rebounds and 7 assists. "He really controlled the tempo," Miller said.[8]

It was nothing new for Kidd. As far back as anyone could remember, he usually was the "go-to guy" in basketball games.

GOLDEN BOY

Laser lights beamed across the basketball court. Cheers and music rocked the Oakland Coliseum Arena as the sound system blared an ear-splitting beat.

It was March of 1991, an exciting time in California prep school basketball. At stake was the Division I state championship, in most minds featuring California's best player against California's best team.

The player was Jason Kidd, a guard who had been Mr. Everything for St. Joseph High School of Alameda. He was largely responsible for the team's 30 victories and its Northern California championship. With his awesome scoring, passing, and rebounding skills, the 6-foot-4, 200-pound junior was considered not only the best high school player in California, but the best prep backcourt player in all of America. But could he lift little St. Joseph over Fremont of Los Angeles, a powerhouse from southern California? "It may take the game of Jason Kidd's life," wrote the *San Francisco Examiner*.[1]

The odds were certainly against St. Joseph. A small Division IV school with merely 400 students, St. Joseph had chosen to play its schedule against the bigger Division I schools. Now St. Joseph faced Fremont, the Southern California champions, in a David vs. Goliath scenario. History was also against St. Joseph. A northern California team had never won a Division I title game since the north-south format was adopted in 1981.

As Jason Kidd was preparing for the game, he looked back on the road that had led him here. It did not seem so long ago that he was a kid growing up in northern California hoping to be another Magic Johnson.

"Magic Johnson was one of my idols when I was a kid," Jason later said of the popular Los Angeles Lakers' guard. "I tried to play like him on the playground."[2]

Soccer was actually Kidd's first love. That is,

until he discovered basketball. Kidd was in the third grade when the fourth-grade team needed another player. The fourth-graders asked Kidd to join them. It would not be the last time he would be facing older players on the court.

"I learned how to pass," he said. "I figured the bigger kids would want me on their team if they knew I was more interested in getting them their shot than in putting the ball up myself."[3]

> "Magic Johnson was one of my idols when I was a kid."
>
> —Jason Kidd

Not that he did not score when the chance presented itself. In one Catholic League game as a fourth-grader, Kidd scored 21 of his team's 30 points.

Kidd was born in San Francisco, California, on March 23, 1973, and grew up across the bay in Oakland. Newspapers described Kidd's family as "middle class" and "multicultural." His father, Steve, a black Baptist from Missouri, worked in the airlines industry for thirty-two years before dying of a heart attack in 1998. His mother, Anne, a white Irish Catholic from the Oakland area, worked in the banking industry for four decades. They raised Jason and sisters Denise and Kim on a ranch, complete with horses, in the Hills section of Oakland.

Jason seemed born to play basketball. At first it

was shooting at the eight-foot rims at Grass Valley Elementary School. By the eighth grade, he was already playing in pickup games against top college players at places like Mosswood Park. That included fellow Oakland resident Gary Payton, who was raised in the so-called "Flats" section that one newspaper described as "the meaner side of town."[4]

"When I first got to him, he was one of these soft little kids," Payton recalled. "He was just beating up on all the little kids his age, and then I really put the ghetto into him."[5]

Those hard-fought pickup games proved to be an education for Kidd. "I learned from being abused by the older guys," Kidd said. "I never quit."[6]

By the time Kidd reached high school he already was a well-known basketball player. In the summer before his freshman season, Kidd played in pick-up games before packed gymnasiums that included top college coaches. In time, Kidd created so much interest that the St. Joseph Pilots were forced to move their games to the Oakland Coliseum to accommodate the larger crowds. They would often draw as many as 11,000 fans—a staggering figure for a high school basketball game.

"Jason put our school on the map," said St. Joseph coach Frank LaPorte.[7]

At the same time, Kidd was putting his likeness on T-shirts, caps, and posters. LaPorte thought it was one good way of marketing Kidd as a local cult hero. Also, it helped to raise money for team road trips. Talk about doing it all for his team, Kidd was up at the crack of dawn to sell donuts in the gym at 7:00 A.M. and autographing rubber basketballs to be auctioned at a pancake breakfast.

His game, meanwhile, was anything but pancake-flat. After two years as a northern California high school phenomenon, Kidd burst into the national spotlight. It happened with a dazzling performance at the prestigious Nike Invitational Basketball Camp the summer before Kidd's junior year. One national prep reporter called Kidd the "premier point guard prospect in the nation."[8] Few would disagree.

So far Kidd had done everything for the Pilots—everything, that is, but win the California state championship. Now, in the 1990–91 season, he hoped to do just that. The Pilots looked awesome. Twice they beat Bishop O'Dowd, St. Joseph's archrival in the East Shore Athletic League. In the past, O'Dowd had dominated St. Joseph. But suddenly the Pilots had turned the tables on their rivals. For Kidd, it was personal. A couple of years before, Kidd had

Jason Kidd guards Gary Payton during a playoff game between the Nets and Milwaukee Bucks in April 2003.

decided to attend St. Joseph instead of O'Dowd because he liked the atmosphere of a smaller school. Now he was showing on a basketball court that bigger was not necessarily better.

The next time Kidd's team met O'Dowd was in the playoffs. Once again, Kidd dominated as St. Joseph won 75–59 to clinch the Northern California Division I championship.

The biggest challenge for Kidd was yet to come: the state championship game against Fremont, the top-ranked team in California. The teams took the court as 14,508 fans rocked the Oakland Coliseum Arena.

Both teams had trouble finding the basket at first. Kidd, especially, was having problems. Facing pressure from multiple defenders, the St. Joseph star managed to sink only one of his first seven shots. Fremont took a 21–15 halftime lead and extended it to 10 points in the second half.

The Pilots finally woke up, tying the game with a 10–0 rally. Back came the Pathfinders, who took a 50–45 lead in the fourth quarter. The game seesawed toward the final minutes. Kidd was playing with four fouls, yet never more aggressively. One more foul and he would be out of the game. No matter.

He was in the middle of everything, making steals, picking off rebounds, and blocking shots.

It was a one-point lead for St. Joseph when Kidd rebounded a missed shot by Fremont, raced the length of the court and fired in a seven-foot jumper. St. Joseph held on to win, 67–61. The Pilots had made California high school basketball history! They were the first Northern California team ever to win the state championship. All thanks to Kidd's last-quarter rescue job. He had scored 9 of his game-high 25 points in the fourth quarter. In addition, he had 8 rebounds, 7 steals, 4 assists, and a blocked shot in a typical all-around game. "Kidd is a fantastic ballplayer who carried his team and won them a championship," said Fremont coach Sam Sullivan.[9]

With Kidd coming back for his senior year, the Pilots were favored to repeat as state champions in 1992. Kidd had created a storm of recruiting interest from top colleges around the country. There was so much attention that coach LaPorte limited phone calls from coaches to the last Sunday of each month. Finally, before the start of his senior season, Kidd made his decision. He was going to the University of California at Berkeley. He would stay close to home.

Kidd was relieved. No more phone calls from coaches. No more questions from reporters about his future. All he had to worry about was winning another state championship.

Everywhere Kidd went, he was the focus of attention. When St. Joseph played in a tournament in Florida, the game program called Kidd the No. 1 player in America. Living up to his billing, Kidd scored 21 points, handed out 13 assists, and made 10 steals as St. Joseph beat Butler of Huntsville,

As a high school junior in 1991, Jason Kidd led his team to the California state basketball championship by defeating Fremont High, 67–61, before 14,508 fans at the Oakland Coliseum Arena.

Alabama, 68–55. Then he scored 32 points in a 67–64 loss to St. Raymond from the Bronx, New York.

There were not many losses for St. Joseph that season. As expected, the Pilots found themselves back in the California Interscholastic Federation (CIF) playoffs and, once again, in the Division 1 championship game. This time the opponent was Mater Dei, which had four times the student population of St. Joseph and had won the state title in 1987 and 1990.

The demand for tickets was great. Many of the 15,788 at ARCO Arena in Sacramento showed up to watch Kidd play his final high school game. He went out a winner as St. Joseph beat Mater Dei 59–37 for its second straight state championship. "I wish we could have kept on playing," Kidd said, "because I didn't want my high school career to end."[10]

Neither did many fans in the arena. They gave Kidd a standing ovation as he walked to the bench with his team leading 57–34. It was the end of a glorious high school career, capped by the USA Today Player of the Year award. In his four years, Kidd had led his high school to an incredible 120–11 record and two state championships.

"Jason went out with a bang," Coach LaPorte said. "He's lived up to every expectation and he never has let us down in a big ballgame."[11]

3

A GOLDEN BEAR

It was suddenly the Jason Kidd Show at the University of California. The arrival of Kidd on the Berkeley campus immediately signaled a new era in Cal basketball. He was just a nineteen-year-old freshman, but everyone expected him to turn the Golden Bears into a national power. It was scary.

Cal was usually one of the worst teams in the Pac-10. The Golden Bears had made only two NCAA playoff appearances since 1960. Now with Kidd in 1992, Cal was established as a contender for national honors. Kidd brashly predicted the Bears would be in the NCAA's Final Four in two years.

Cal had an early test against Wake Forest, a team from the highly regarded Atlantic Coast Conference.

There was a lot of interest in the game. So much so that it had to be moved from Cal's small Harmon Arena on campus to the Oakland Coliseum Arena. More than 15,000 tickets were sold. Many more fans were glued to their television sets watching the game on cable.

Here is what they saw:

Cal was leading 43–39 with 15 minutes left when Kidd took a high pass just over the half-court line. Twisting his body in the air like an acrobat, Kidd redirected the ball with a masterful touch pass to Lamond Murray for a slam dunk.

Kidd then forced a turnover and hit Ryan Jamison with a sharp pass for another easy score. Again, it was Wake Forest ball. Again, it was Kidd disrupting things. This time he deflected the ball away from the Demon Deacons and then piled into the stands as the ball sailed out of bounds.

Kidd's aggressive play sparked roars from the sell-out crowd. It also sparked his team.

"It fired us up," said Murray of Kidd's spurt that led the Bears to an 81–65 victory.[1]

Suddenly, Cal was undefeated at 5–0 and the talk of college basketball. "The Bay Area has been a college hoop graveyard ever since San Francisco commanded the rankings 15 seasons ago," wrote the *Orange*

County Register. "Jason Kidd, not even a month into his career, has moved the axis."[2]

But hold on—the Bears were a relatively inexperienced team that included nine freshmen and sophomores among its twelve players. How far could they move the "axis"? As the season wore on, the Bears continued to answer that question with the "axis" revolving around Kidd. After Kidd led Cal to a 104–82 thrashing of UCLA at the Bruins' Pauley Pavilion, UCLA coaching legend John Wooden, who had won ten NCAA championships, was impressed. "This is the best I've seen a Cal team play against UCLA since the days of Pete Newell," said Wooden, referring to Cal's national champions of 1959.[3]

The University of Washington had to be feeling the same way after losing to Cal 79–65. Kidd literally stole the show with 8 steals that broke a Cal mark and tied the Pac-10 record.

Not all went smoothly for the Bears, however. There was suddenly a succession of losses in the middle of the season that put Cal's NCAA tournament chances in jeopardy. And then there was the firing of coach Lou Campanelli, who reportedly had been at odds with his players. "With all the adversity we've all been through, we have a long way to go to get

Cal point guard Jason Kidd brings the ball upcourt during a Pac-10 conference game against the Washington State Cougars.

where we want to be, which is the tournament," Kidd said.[4]

Todd Bozeman took over as coach. Many of the players were happier. Kidd had often talked to his father about how hard it was to play for Campanelli. "The biggest thing is everybody is relaxed—there's no tension," Kidd said after Campanelli was fired.[5]

The Cal team was focused on one goal in the winter of 1993: an NCAA tournament bid. Kidd figured the Bears had to win at least six more games to do it. They did better—they won eight of their last nine. A couple of days after Kidd led the Bears to a 78–72 win over Oregon State on the last day of the regular season, the NCAA came calling. The Bears were in the NCAAs for only the third time in thirty-four years.

For Jason Kidd, it was thrilling. As a youth, Kidd used to watch his idol Magic Johnson perform magically on TV. Now Kidd wanted to make some magic of his own. Like Johnson, Kidd was the main ball handler on his team. He was the one who determined the flow of the game. Everything rested on the shoulders of this freshman guard.

But Kidd was a freshman in name only. He had been through a long and grueling season that

In his freshman year at Cal, Jason Kidd led the basketball team into the NCAA tournament for just the third time in thirty-four years.

included a lot of ups and downs. Going into the NCAAs he was as cool and confident as any senior.

With a game on the line, Kidd wanted to have the ball in his hands. LSU was Cal's first test in the NCAAs. The game was tied at 64 with 22 seconds left. Up court with the ball came Kidd, faking out defenders right and left. "I was expecting them to foul me immediately," he said. But suddenly, Kidd saw an opening. "I was looking to pass, but when I saw the opening I went to the lane."[6]

All of a sudden, Kidd drove to the basket and scooped in a twisting shot with 1.5 seconds left. Final: Cal 66, LSU 64. "It was a pretzel shot," said LSU coach Dale Brown. "I don't know how he did it."[7]

Brown also did not know how Cal was going to beat its next opponent, Duke. "I don't think they have a prayer against Duke," he said.[8]

That's what others thought as well. With two straight national championships, the Blue Devils were heavy favorites to win another. Most interesting was how Kidd would match up against Bobby Hurley, Duke's senior point guard. Like Kidd, Hurley was the catalyst on his team. But Hurley already had two NCAA titles under his belt. The Blue Devils also featured Grant Hill, also one of the country's finest college players.

For most of the game at the Rosemont Horizon arena in Rosemont, Illinois, it was no contest. Except it was Cal, not Duke, that had the upper hand. Sparked by Kidd, Cal led by 10 points at the half, 18 early in the second half and then by 17 with about 13 minutes remaining.

Suddenly, Hurley, Grant Hill, and Thomas Hill brought the Blue Devils to life. Duke chopped away at Cal's huge lead. They finally tied the game at 76 on Hurley's three-point shot with 3:55 remaining. The Blue Devils edged ahead 77–76 on Thomas Hill's free throw with 2:21 left.

The Bears had given up control of a game they had held for most of the night. With 17,463 fans roaring, the game appropriately came down to a confrontation between Kidd and Hurley.

With Hurley hounding him, Kidd quickly brought the ball up court along the left baseline. Kidd tried a pass, but it was deflected by Hurley. Loose ball near the basket. "I thought I had a steal," Hurley said later.[9] Somehow, Kidd managed to follow up his own pass and retrieve the ball from under a tangle of bodies. Kidd went up and fired a spinning shot into the basket. He was fouled by Grant Hill and converted

Kidd talks with University of California Head Coach Lou Campanelli during a timeout in a game in January 1992.

the free throw. It was Cal by two points, and the Bears hung on to win, 82–77.

"Hurley went for the steal [and knocked the ball free], but I continued to follow my pass," Kidd said. "It just bounced my way. I grabbed it. I had one thought. That was to score a basket. That stopped their run."[10]

Hurley had done his best to keep Duke's season alive, scoring a game-high 32 points. But Kidd was every bit as good in his own way with 11 points, 14 assists, and 8 rebounds—nearly a triple-double (double figures in three offensive categories). Not to mention his clutch play with the game up for grabs at the end.

Cal fans were celebrating, chanting and pointing to the sports writers on press row. Their message: The California Golden Bears are better than you guys thought, eh?

After sparking one of Cal's greatest victories in the school's history, Kidd came crashing down to earth in a loss to Kansas. But Kidd had delivered his message to the college basketball world: As a freshman, he had been as good as everyone had expected, maybe better. The college basketball world, and particularly Cal fans, could not wait to see what happened next.

4

THE NEXT LEVEL

Will he or won't he? That was the most-asked question in 1994 about Jason Kidd as he led Cal to another NCAA tournament. Everyone was wondering if Kidd would stay in school for another year or leave after the season for the NBA.

After a late-season victory over Oregon, fans chanted "One more year!" to Kidd and teammate Lamond Murray, who also had college eligibility left. "That's good they want me to come back," Kidd said, "but I haven't made my decision."[1]

But everyone else in the basketball world seemed to think it was a slam dunk: Kidd would soon join the pros.

Almost single-handedly, he had turned around

the Cal basketball program. In two short years, the Bears had gone from perennial whipping boys in the Pac-10 to the team holding the whip—or more precisely, Jason Kidd controlling the ball.

He was the main reason the Bears were in the NCAA tournament for the second straight year. Game after game during the 1993–94 season, Kidd put on one dazzling performance after another. And the Bears were piling up victories over teams that used to dominate them.

Facing Oregon late in the season, Kidd simply took over the game with a typical display during the first 10 minutes. The following action at Cal's Harmon gym had the makings of a highlight reel that would make pro teams drool:

Kidd blocks a shot. He fires an alley-oop pass to Lamond Murray for a dunk. He sneaks in to tie up an Oregon player for a jump ball. He hits a fall-away jumper from the baseline. He throws a spectacular pass. He hits a three-point jumper. He fires another stunning pass that a teammate fails to convert. He scores on a slam dunk after a teammate's steal. He makes a steal and passes to Akili Jones for a layup. He hits a jumper in the lane. Then a fall-away three-point jumper. Then he steals the ball to set up a dunk by Murray.

After Cal's 82–73 victory, the *San Francisco Chronicle* wrote: "the crowd was dazzled, and it looked like Kidd might shower at halftime and get himself drafted by an NBA team before the evening was over."[2]

Not quite, but the inevitable happened as soon as the season was over. Following a shocking loss to Wisconsin-Green Bay in the NCAA tournament, Kidd made his less than shocking announcement: He was giving up the final two years of his college eligibility to become a pro.

The twenty-one-year-old Kidd admittedly was still learning the game and had to improve his outside shooting for the NBA. Nevertheless, NBA teams were excited about his all-around talent and his court vision—his ability to "see" the floor. His skill at setting up scoring chances with his uncanny passes and controlling a game with his ball-handling drew comparisons to Isiah Thomas and Magic Johnson, the player Kidd most admired. In his time at Cal, Kidd had set single-season assist records in the Pac-10, leading the nation with 9.1 a game during the 1993–94 season. He was equally as skilled on defense. In just 59 games, he became Cal's career steal leader.

In the 1994 NBA draft, Kidd was among a rich

crop of collegians available that included Purdue's Glenn Robinson and Duke's Grant Hill.

The Dallas Mavericks, with the second pick, selected Kidd after the Milwaukee Bucks picked Robinson. The Mavericks had seen what Kidd had done to turn around a college team. Now they hoped he could do the same for them. They needed a lot of help. For two straight seasons, the Mavericks were the worst team in the NBA.

"Hopefully I can do what I think I'm capable of doing for this team and that's taking leadership right off the bat and directing this team back to where it's capable of being," Kidd said after signing a nine-year, $60 million contract.[3]

But Kidd also had to get his personal life moving in the right direction. On the court, he was close to perfect. This was not so much the case away from basketball.

He was in trouble with the law for two incidents: In 1994 he faced misdemeanor hit-and-run and speeding charges for a high-speed collision involving his car on an Oakland freeway. He also faced a suit by an eighteen-year-old woman who claimed Kidd assaulted her during a party at his Oakland home.

Also, his first impression on Dallas coach Dick Motta was anything but positive. Motta was angry that Kidd had skipped a voluntary mini-camp in July. Kidd did appear in a September mini-camp, but only after signing his contract.

All was pretty much forgotten in the Mavericks' camp once Kidd started to play. As early as the first exhibition contests, Kidd was already putting his personal stamp on games. With Dallas leading Indiana by six points with about three minutes left, Kidd was not content just to slow down the game and protect the lead. He continued to push the ball down court and find teammates for easy baskets. "We have to keep running, no matter what the score is," Kidd said after the 103–91 victory. "That's going to be our game—push the ball and get easy baskets. I love to get the ball up and down like that."[4]

> "Hopefully, I can do what I'm capable of . . . and that's taking leadership right off the bat."
> —Jason Kidd

It did not take Kidd long to make a true believer of Motta. "Jason has a true work ethic and great instincts to go where the ball is and [know] what the opposition is going to do," the Dallas coach said.[5]

On opening night the Mavericks faced the New Jersey Nets at sold-out Reunion Arena. The crowd of 17,502 was there to see the start of the Jason Kidd era in Dallas, and Kidd would not disappoint.

Jason Kidd leads his Dallas Mavericks teammates on a fast break during a game on December 10, 1996.

Although he only managed to make 3 of 10 shots and score 10 points, he lit up the arena with other facets of his game. He handed out 11 assists, grabbed 9 rebounds, and made 3 steals. "Forget the 3-for-10," wrote the *Dallas Morning News* after the Mavericks' 112–103 triumph. "Young Jason had Reunion reeling with a variety of razzle-dazzle passes that not only produced 11 assists, but also seemed to energize his teammates."[6]

It had been a long time since there was anything for Mavericks fans to cheer about. Now with Kidd starring alongside Jim Jackson and Jamal Mashburn in a very young lineup, the Mavericks were suddenly filling their arena with excitement and their season with victories. Kidd continued to impress in a variety of ways.

Playing in just his fourteenth NBA game one month later, Kidd and his teammates trailed the San Antonio Spurs by one point with 22.8 seconds left. With the Spurs in possession, the game seemed to be all but lost for the Mavericks. During a timeout huddle, a teammate said to Kidd: "Work your magic, Jason, we've got to have the ball."[7]

As if scripted, Kidd jumped in front of the Spurs' inbound pass at half court and deflected the ball, then chased it as it rolled toward the sidelines. In an amazing display of athleticism, Kidd scooped up the ball just before going out of bounds. While still in the air, he called a 20-second timeout by putting his hands on his shoulders before hitting the floor. Significantly, Kidd was aware that the 20-second timeout was the only one the Mavericks had left. Had he called a regular timeout, the ball would have been handed back to the Spurs. The Mavericks tied the game and went on to win in overtime.

From the start of the season, the NBA's Rookie of the Year prize was considered Grant Hill's to lose. The popular, high-profile player from Duke now playing for Detroit was all but penciled in for the award by the nation's sportswriters and sportscasters. Robinson, having a good season as well, was also penciled in as Hill's chief challenger. That is, until Kidd put on a dazzling late-season surge, waking up the media that hadn't been paying too much attention to the persistent Dallas guard. Suddenly, it was a three-player, down-to-the-wire race for the rookie prize.

On April 5, Kidd scored 19 points along with 10 rebounds, and 12 assists against the Los Angeles Lakers for a "triple-double"—double figures in three offensive categories.

Two nights later, Kidd did it again—11 points,

Kidd prepares to put up a shot during a game against the Indiana Pacers in 1995.

10 rebounds and 13 assists against Minnesota. "How many point guards are capable of triple-doubles?" coach Motta said. "Not very many."[8] In fact, the last to do it was Magic Johnson, in 1991.

And Kidd was not finished. In a thrilling double-overtime 156–147 victory over defending NBA champion Houston, Kidd rattled off 38 points, 11 rebounds, and 10 assists.

With his late explosion, Kidd had suddenly turned around the race for the Rookie of the Year, just as he had turned around the Mavericks' entire season. When the votes were counted, Kidd and Hill wound up in a tie for the award.

In recognizing Kidd, the media noticed the impact he had on his team. With Kidd directing the offense and stabilizing the defense, the Mavericks had improved their record by a remarkable 23 games. Although they failed to make the playoffs, they were not eliminated until the last week of the season.

Kidd's first season as a professional had been a rousing success. Just as he had in college, he had turned his team around.

5

ALL-STAR
KIDD

Jason Kidd stood in the wings waiting to hear his name announced. Then he raced onto the court as thousands cheered. Kidd smiled and waved.

It was February 11, 1996, and Kidd was playing in his first NBA All-Star Game. Only in his second year in the league, he had been picked to start at one of the guard positions for the Western Conference. It was the first time in the Dallas Mavericks' sixteen-year history that one of their players had started in an All-Star Game. Kidd was as excited as he was nervous.

"I didn't want to embarrass myself," he said. "I didn't want to let my teammates down."[1]

Not everyone felt Kidd belonged in the starting

Jason Kidd streaks past his defender as he pushes the ball up court for the Phoenix Suns.

lineup. Seattle coach George Karl was openly critical of the fans' choice. He said Utah's John Stockton and his own Gary Payton "are a helluva lot better than him."[2] Kidd had actually outplayed both of them in head-to-head meetings right before the All-Star Game. Facing Stockton, the NBA's all-time assist leader, Kidd came out on top with a Reunion Arena record 25 assists.

Now it was the All-Star Game in San Antonio, Texas. Kidd was hoping to prove his worth as a legitimate All-Star. He said he and Karl had "kissed and made up."[3] It was literally the truth. Karl had planted a kiss on Kidd's cheek during media interviews. Karl would be coaching Kidd's West team and had nothing but praise for the Dallas All-Star.

Suddenly, it was "showtime," and Kidd was showing the crowd of 36,037 at the Alamodome what he could do: In just nine minutes of play in the first quarter, Kidd made a couple of steals and assisted on five baskets. The assists featured a spectacular "no-look" pass from center court that set up a dunk shot for Shawn Kemp and brought the crowd and teammates to their feet.

By the end of the game, Kidd had recorded a game-high 10 assists, scored 7 points, and grabbed 6 rebounds in just 22 minutes. No matter that his

West team was beaten 129–118, Kidd had shown he was a star among stars. "I love Jason Kidd," said fellow All-Star Charles Barkley. "I'd pay to see him play."[4]

Back in Dallas, you would not hear the same praise from Jimmy Jackson. He and Kidd, in a dispute over team leadership, had stopped talking to each other. Said *Sports Illustrated*: "First Kidd questioned JJ's desire to win, then he demonstrated his own commitment to the team by demanding that either he or Jackson be traded."[5]

"The [rift] obviously drew a lot of attention . . . and it affected a young team," said Dallas vice president of basketball operations Keith Grant.[6]

But the Mavericks had hoped to hold on to Jason and Jackson, along with Jamal Mashburn. They were planning to build their future around the so-called "three Js," whom they considered franchise players. They had committed $106 million in contracts to the talented trio. But with all the bickering, plus an injury to Mashburn, the Mavericks went into a season-long slump and never recovered.

Despite the team's bad season, it was a good one for Kidd individually. He averaged 16.6 points a game, and his 9.7 assists were good for second in the league. "After just two NBA seasons," wrote *Sports*

Jason Kidd looks to pass while being guarded by Terry Dehere of the Los Angeles Clippers during a game in February 1997.

Illustrated, "he's on the verge of becoming the best point guard in the league. His genius for playmaking has been compared to that of Bob Cousy and Magic Johnson."[7]

Kidd's days in Dallas were numbered, nevertheless. Early in the 1996–97 season, the Mavericks traded him to the Phoenix Suns in a six-player deal. Kidd was relieved. "Basketball just wasn't fun for me anymore," he said.[8]

Kidd was anxious to show his stuff to the Phoenix fans. However, he was sidelined by a fractured collarbone in his very first game with his new team. He was out of action for fifty days. Finally, he was reactivated in the middle of February.

Early in March the Suns traveled to Dallas. Kidd faced his former team for the first time since the December 26 trade. The fans at Reunion Arena booed him at the beginning of the game. When he missed a free throw, they cheered. When he had the ball stolen from him, the fans shouted insults.

The Suns fell behind the Mavericks by 27 points in the third quarter. No way they could come back. Or could they? The Suns started a rally. And guess who was leading the charge? None other than Jason Kidd. The Suns forced overtime.

Again, the Suns faced an uphill fight. With just a

Kidd puts up a shot against a Bulls defender during a game in Chicago in December 1997.

few seconds left in overtime, they trailed the Mavericks by one point. Suddenly, Kidd drove the lane. He found Wayman Tisdale open and flipped a pass. Tisdale scored on a layup with just two seconds left. Remarkably, the Suns pulled out a 109–108 victory. Kidd celebrated the winning basket by raising two clenched fists and jumping into the arms of Kevin Johnson, his veteran backcourt teammate. "I never thought the game was over," said Kidd, who scored 23 points. "I just kept telling the team, 'Stay with me. Stay with me.' "[9]

It was a timely victory for the Suns, who, amazingly enough, were now in the race for a playoff berth. Who would have thought that was possible after beginning the season with an 0–13 record? No NBA team had ever made the playoffs after starting the season with thirteen straight losses. At one point in mid-February the Suns were actually sixteen games below .500. But late in the season, the Suns were suddenly turning things around.

At one point they put together an eleven-game winning streak to clinch a playoff berth. And Kidd was given the credit for the Suns' incredible comeback. "In the first game he was in, in one half, we saw a completely different basketball team," said Phoenix assistant coach Donn Nelson. "It was the most amazing metamorphosis that I personally have seen."[10]

Nothing changed in the playoffs, however. After beating Seattle 106–101 behind Kidd in the playoff opener, the Suns were soon bounced out in the first round. The trend continued in 1998, even though they had won 16 more games in the regular season. In 1999, the Suns were knocked out of the playoffs again following a magical season by Kidd. He averaged a league-leading 10.8 assists and a guards-best 6.8 rebounds. In addition, Kidd's seven triple-doubles almost matched the combined total of the rest of the league, which had nine.

For some time Kidd's dream had been to play on the U.S. Olympic basketball team. In 1996 he had come close. Finally, success! Kidd's dream came true when he made the roster for the so-called "Dream Team" that would play in the 2000 Olympics in Australia. After several great seasons in Phoenix, the choice of Kidd was justified. He had established himself as one of the league's top point guards. He had become an All-Star who was more concerned with setting up his teammates for baskets than scoring himself.

Sometimes his passes were spectacular, sometimes extremely simple, but always on the mark.

Kidd dishes off a no-look pass during a playoff game against the San Antonio Spurs in 1998.

And they usually ended in a basket. One play against the Houston Rockets, which had become typically routine for Kidd, exemplified his great ability to pass a basketball:

Kidd drives from the right into the lane and leaps into the air. Two Houston players go up with Kidd to stop his apparent shot attempt. No such luck. Kidd spots Clifford Robinson open and whips an over-the-shoulder pass to him. Slam dunk!

"Jason is the NBA's most exciting playmaker," said *Sports Illustrated*.[11]

Fast-forward to the 2000 NBA All-Star Game. Once again, Kidd showed off his extraordinary passing skills in the wide-open game. This time, he led all players with 14 assists to trigger a 137–126 win for the West over the East. Who was the best guard in basketball now?

The spectacular show was becoming commonplace for Kidd. He had led his team into the NBA playoffs all three seasons he had been in Phoenix. Now all he had to figure out was how to get the Suns past the first round.

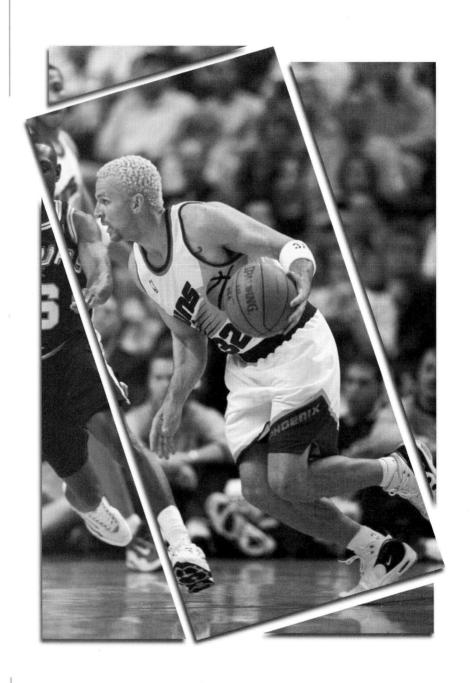

BUMPY SEASON, BREAKOUT GAME

Late in the 1999–2000 season the news flashed across the nation's television screens: Jason Kidd was severely injured. He had suffered a broken left ankle in a game against the Sacramento Kings.

The medical report was not good. At the very least, Kidd would not be able to play for the rest of the regular season. And, a team spokesman added, Kidd "was questionable for the playoffs."[1]

The Phoenix Suns were battling for a playoff spot. Now they would have to do it without Kidd. He would be unable to play for the first time since becoming a Sun in 1996. Everyone was concerned, from Kidd's teammates to just about every basketball fan in Phoenix.

Such bad news was not unexpected in Phoenix that season. The Suns had been plagued by a run of bad luck: the resignation of the head coach, the near-death of a player, and the loss of many of their top players to injury for long periods of time.

Remarkably, the Suns not only stayed in the thick of the playoff race, but boasted one of the best records in the NBA. It had been "an unbelievably crazy year," said Scott Skiles, who had taken over the coaching job after Danny Ainge resigned on December 13. "I don't think I've ever seen anything like it."[2]

Losing Kidd was the final blow. The Suns' unquestioned team leader, he was leading the NBA in assists and averaging 14.5 points a game. How could the Suns replace such a player?

But the Suns somehow finished tied for the fourth-best record in the Western Conference. It was all good news in the first round of the playoffs as the Suns won two of the first three games against defending NBA champion San Antonio. One more victory in the best-of-five series and the Suns would advance to the second round.

Things were going well for the Suns. Suddenly it got better: Kidd was returning.

He had been all but forgotten in the Suns' playoff

drive and their early success in the postseason. But seeing their teammate back on the court gave the Suns an emotional lift.

"When they announced that Jason was going to play, the team went crazy," said Penny Hardaway, who with Kidd formed one of the most potent backcourt duos in the league. "I was so happy because I knew he was going to make my job easier."[3]

It was business as usual. Sporting a new blond hairdo and playing with two screws in his left ankle, Kidd led the Suns to an 89–78 win over the Spurs. The Suns were in the second round for the first time in five years!

"It was incredible to have him back," Suns guard Kevin Johnson said of Kidd. "His energy just carried over to everybody."[4]

But not enough to produce a victory in the first three games against the powerful Los Angeles Lakers. Now in Game 4, it was win or go home for the Suns. Kidd had played well for the most part, but struggled mightily with his shooting in Game 3. He played 40 minutes despite a sore ankle, even diving into the press table in the final minute. He knew he had to lift his game for the Suns to have any chance at all against a great Lakers team led by Shaquille O'Neal and Kobe Bryant.

Jason Kidd sports his blonde hair during the 2000 playoffs against the San Antonio Spurs.

Though down, the Suns believed they were not out. "We won 53 games and did that with one of our players (Tom Gugliotta, who had a seizure on the team bus in December) almost dying, a coaching change and injuries," Kidd said. "That just shows the character of this team."[5]

In Game 4, Kidd hit a three-pointer to give the Suns an early lead. He banked in another while racing down court. Kidd was also setting up teammates for shots. By the half, he had accumulated 16 points and 12 assists—as many assists as the entire Lakers team combined. The Suns led by 23 points at the half, and then 29 in the third period.

"He was phenomenal," Suns coach Skiles said of Kidd. "He was all over the court, pushing the ball, making great decisions. Anybody who was open, he got them the ball, and he knocked down his shots."[6]

What sore ankle?

"I felt like I could push the ball, and my legs felt good," Kidd said. "My ankle's not bothering me, and the shot was dropping."[7]

After going 1-for-9 in Game 3, Kidd went 8-for-13 in Game 4. He dealt a blow to the Lakers in one thirty-seven-second span in the third period with a rebound, assist, steal and three-pointer. The Suns won going away, 117–98, to stay alive in the playoffs.

Kidd attempts to block the shot of Spurs point guard Avery Johnson during a playoff game against San Antonio in 2000.

Jason's numbers told the story: a career-high 16 assists, 22 points, and 10 rebounds. It was his first triple-double in the postseason.

The season ended all too soon for Phoenix as the Lakers ultimately prevailed. But the Suns did not hang their heads in defeat. Throughout the season they had shown just what a proud team could accomplish under the most adverse circumstances. And Kidd had shown what it took to be a leader in the face of even more adversity.

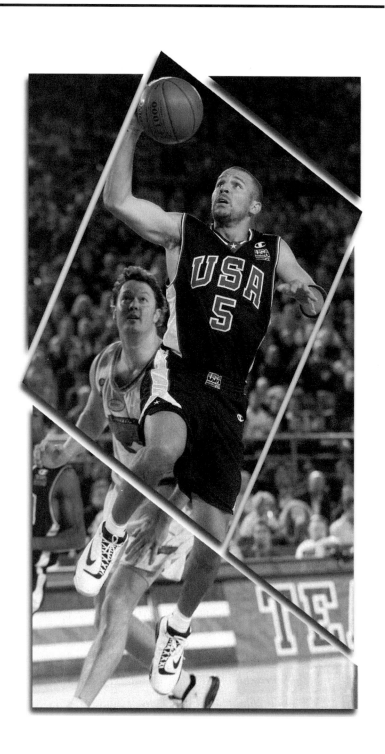

7

GOLDEN

Jason Kidd was in Hawaii, but it was hardly a vacation. While most everyone else was out on the beach or in a cool air-conditioned hotel or restaurant, he was working up a sweat in a hot gymnasium.

Not that Kidd minded. He and other NBA stars were preparing to play in the 2000 Olympics in Australia.

"If you were to watch how tough the practices have been here, you would think we were trying to make a team and not already be on a team," Kidd said.[1]

Of course, Kidd was already a member of the United States basketball team that was hoping to bring home another gold medal from the international games. In fact, he was actually tri-captain of the team along with Alonzo Mourning and boyhood pal Gary Payton.

"I'm really excited," Kidd said. "As a kid you always dream about representing your country. Being able to watch the first Dream Team in '92, then in '96, that's when I pushed a little harder to be on the team because I always wanted to represent my country."[2]

It would be hard for the 2000 Olympic team to match up to the 1992 team, in both performance and star power. The Americans that year featured such legendary NBA players as Michael Jordan, Magic Johnson, and Larry Bird. They breezed to an Olympic gold medal in Barcelona by an average margin of 44 points. The 1996 team—unofficially called "Dream Team II"—was not too bad, either. That team crushed all opponents by a 32-point average en route to another gold medal.

At two Olympics, the Americans had established a pattern: They were not only expected to win, but win big. By 2000, things had changed. The Americans, who had never lost a game since NBA players first participated in the Olympics in 1992, were no longer held in awe by opponents. So many good foreign players were now in the NBA that they made their countries' teams much stronger.

When the third edition of the U.S. team was announced for the 2000 Olympics, some of the biggest names in the NBA were missing. Instead, the exclusive squad of twelve included many names that were unfamiliar to the international community. Prior to the team's final workout before the start of the Olympic grind, an Australian newspaper pointed out that many of the Americans' "A-list" players were not on the team. The newspaper disrespectfully referred to Kidd as "Jason who?"

> "I'm really excited. As a kid you always dream about representing your country."
> —Jason Kidd, on playing in the Olympics

"Some people say that we don't have our best players here," Kidd said. "We have to prove to them that some of the best players are here."[3]

Not that the Americans were not still the favorites to win the gold medal. In five tune-up games for the Olympics, they had won by an average of 35 points. "Our biggest competition will be ourselves," said Mourning. "Nobody is going to come close to the challenges we have had against each other."[4]

Perhaps. But the Lithuanians gave Team USA a real battle before losing by 9 points in a preliminary-round game. It was the Americans' closest call in the opening round. And it was a harbinger of things to come when the U.S. again faced Lithuania in the medal round. The winner would go to the gold medal game.

The Americans led by 12 points at halftime. But Lithuania chipped away at the lead. And with the clock ticking down to the final seconds, the Lithuanians had the opportunity to pull off one of the greatest upsets in sports history.

Trailing the U.S. team by merely two points, Lithuania had a chance to win when Sarunas Jasikevicius took a shot at the buzzer from behind the three-point line. But the shot fell short and the Americans, breathing a collective sigh of relief, held on to win, 85–83. "I think twelve guys would have changed their identities [had the U.S. lost]," said Kidd, who was guarding Jasikevicius and careful not to foul him and give the Lithuanian star another chance at the free-throw line.[5]

The gold medal game against France was another thriller. The French-dominated crowd chanted, "Allez les bleus." Translation: "Go Blue." Meanwhile the red, white, and blue of the United States struggled to

Jason Kidd shows his Olympic Gold Medal to his young son T.J. after the U.S. defeated France, 85–75.

hold on to a slim lead. With less than five minutes left, the French had cut the Americans' lead to just four points, 76–72. Finally, the Americans pulled away for an 85–75 victory. "We had to work hard for the gold medal," Kidd said. "It wasn't just handed to us, and that makes it special."[6]

Kidd had played a vital part for the U.S. Olympic team. Back home, he was ready to do the same for the Phoenix Suns. Kidd had earned a vacation. Instead, he joined the Suns' training camp right after the Olympics.

Kidd was anxious to start his seventh NBA season. No wonder. At age twenty-seven, he was at the top of his game. "Anyone who wants to learn to play point guard should study Jason Kidd," said Mike Bibby, then of the Vancouver Grizzlies.[7]

Kidd's private life was hardly going as smoothly. En route to his best season, he suddenly became the center of a shocking news story. Kidd was arrested on suspicion of domestic abuse. Kidd's wife, Joumana, told police that Kidd had hit her during an argument at home. Police said Kidd admitted hitting her. He was going to court, facing a misdemeanor assault charge.

The story stunned the entire basketball community. The Kidds had been considered the ideal pro sports couple, and with their son, T.J., the ideal family. The player and his wife operated the Jason Kidd Foundation, which contributed to local children's charities. Kidd had credited his wife with helping his rise to basketball stardom. He would blow kisses to her every time he prepared to shoot from the foul line.

The Phoenix Suns called a news conference. Kidd appeared along with team owner Jerry Colangelo to make a public apology. "I love my wife," Kidd said. "I love my family. This is a situation that is embarrassing to me, to my family, my friends, and also to the Phoenix Suns."[8]

Kidd blows a kiss to his wife from the free throw line as he prepares to put up his shot.

When Kidd next played at home, he went on radio to apologize to the Suns' fans and ask their forgiveness. "That will never happen again," he said.[9] Then he wrote a letter to season ticket holders, apologizing once more. Dealing with fans when the Suns were on the road was another matter. He was taunted in many cities around the NBA. In Boston, fans called him "wife beater."

At every stop in every NBA city, Kidd faced questions from the press. Playing in the All-Star Game, there were more questions. Kidd tried to answer every one as best he could. "I was selected for the All-Star Game," he said. "I'm not going to hide. I was going to face it, that's what life is all about."[10]

Kidd was trying hard to turn his life around. This was a tougher job than any he had faced on the basketball court. Kidd was told by authorities: Stay out of trouble for a year and the assault charge would be dropped. Also, Kidd had to undergo counseling. He and his wife appeared at a news conference. Both looked happy. Holding hands, Jason and Joumana revealed that she was going to have another child.

Kidd obviously had other things on his mind than basketball when he took the court. And the Suns were struggling. With about six weeks left in the season, they were in danger of missing the playoffs.

Bobby Jackson of the Sacramento Kings drives past Jason Kidd during Game 4 of the Kings' first-round playoff series against the Phoenix Suns on May 2, 2001.

They called a players-only meeting. The message to Kidd: Play better, or we will be out of the playoffs.

Kidd did play better. In one three-game stretch, he scored 31, 32, and 36 points. He had never scored more than 30 two games in a row. "It took me a while to get my attitude back," Kidd said. "Having your teammates tell you they need you had a lot to do with it."[11]

The Suns rode Kidd's hot hand right into the playoffs. Down went Sacramento in the first game as Kidd reeled off 18 points and 14 assists. But the Suns' season ended as the Kings won the next three games.

It had been a strange season, with Kidd the headline maker both on and off the court. Soon, he would be making headlines elsewhere. In the off-season, the news hit the NBA like a bombshell: Kidd, the Suns' all-everything player, had been traded to the New Jersey Nets for Stephon Marbury.

Once again, Kidd picked up his family and moved to another NBA team. He could only wonder what fate had in store for him in New Jersey. He never expected what was going to happen. And neither did anyone else.

8

JASON TO THE RESCUE

J ason Kidd faced the biggest challenge of his career. Could he make the troubled New Jersey Nets a contender?

Soon after signing with his new team, he made a bold prediction: The Nets would win 40 games in the 2001–02 season and make the playoffs.

Even his teammates had a hard time believing that. The season before, the Nets had one of the worst records in the league at 26–56. Same old Nets. Since joining the NBA in 1976, the Nets had been one of the worst teams—a poor relative to the far more popular New York Knicks across the river. Filling the arena was almost as difficult as filling the net. The Nets did not have any championships to show for their twenty-five years in the NBA—not even a division title. Just making the playoffs was a big deal. Or winning a playoff series, something the Nets had not accomplished since 1984.

But Kidd was excited as he started training camp. Kidd realized the Nets had many talented players such as Kenyon Martin, Kerry Kittles, Keith Van Horn, and Richard Jefferson. All they had to do was believe in themselves.

Named as one of the co-captains, Kidd told his teammates that things would change. "We're going to communicate," he said. "If we don't, we'll all be in trouble."[1]

Kidd's teammates—and Nets fans—began appreciating his skills soon enough. Early in the season the Nets faced the Phoenix Suns, Kidd's former team. It was the first time that Kidd faced Stephon Marbury since the previous summer's trade. Marbury outscored Kidd, but it did not matter. The Nets won, 106–87. "My goal was to beat them without scoring," said Kidd, who finished with 6 points but had a game-high 13 assists. "I wanted to demonstrate the game in a different light."[2]

Most importantly, the Nets were winning. They were off to the best start in their history. They were on top of the Atlantic Division at the time. And by the middle of January the Nets had the best record in the entire Eastern Conference at 25–11. Kidd's unselfish style of play was starting to pay off in New Jersey. As the main ball handler on the Nets, he was more concerned with setting up teammates for baskets than scoring himself. He also had a calming effect on his team. Kidd was featured on the front cover of *Sports Illustrated*, and his name was starting to be mentioned in MVP talk.

After beating the Knicks at Madison Square Garden, 114–96, the New Jersey players actually heard fans shout, "N-E-T-S! Nets! Nets! Nets!" In previous years, they were lucky to hear such encouragement even at home.

"There's not just one team here [in the New York area] anymore," said Nets coach Byron Scott. "It's not just the Knicks anymore."[3]

Despite the fact that the Nets were on top of the Eastern Conference, there were still skeptics who did not think they belonged there. Sooner or later, they believed, the Nets would revert to the losing habits of past seasons. After all, they said, these were the Nets.

Midway through the 2001–02 season, the Nets faced the San Antonio Spurs in a game that was a true test. Eight days before, the Nets had beaten the

Spurs at home. The Spurs, the NBA champions in 1999, were one of the league's most powerful teams. And now they were looking for revenge.

Kidd, meanwhile, was looking for redemption. Just the day before against Dallas, he had one of his worst shooting games as a pro. Kidd missed his first 15 shots and finished an embarrassing 1 for 17 from the field.

Now against San Antonio, Kidd was all pumped up. He hit his first three shots. Then with a little over a minute left in the fourth quarter, he hit the clincher with a 15-foot shot as the Nets held off the Spurs, 92–86. Kidd finished with 28 points. He also grabbed a team-high 11 rebounds. "That's as big a win as we've had all season," Scott said.[4] The New York newspapers now had something more positive to write about in the metropolitan area than the struggling Knicks.

> "My goal was to beat them without scoring. I wanted to demonstrate the game in a different light."
> —Jason Kidd

The Nets' 28–13 record at the halfway point seemed like a miracle to most basketball people. The Nets had already won two games more than they had the entire season before. And now, Kidd's prediction of a 40-win season seemed ridiculously low. "At

40, maybe the bar was set a little low, but going in blind, we had to start somewhere," Kidd said. "Sometimes you have to raise your goals as your season goes on."[5]

In their twenty-five-year NBA history, the Nets had never won more than 49 games in a season. That was 1982–83, when they went 49–33. Now they had a good chance to make club history as the first New Jersey Nets team to win 50.

Not that the Nets were always amazing. Late in the season, they went into a slump, losing all four games on a West Coast trip. Kidd was booed in Phoenix and was later fined $5,000 for gesturing toward the fans. The Nets finally got back on track with three straight wins at home, where they usually dominated. The Nets beat the Los Angeles Lakers for their 49th win, matching the total of the 1982–83 team. One more to go for the magic number of 50. More importantly, a chance to clinch the Atlantic Division title.

Against Boston, the Nets were not at their best. They fell behind by 19 points and lost at the Continental Airlines Arena. Next up, the Washington Wizards. The Nets had another chance to clinch before their home fans. Kidd and the Nets got off to a fast start. The Nets continued to pour it on in the second half with Kidd leading the way. And the chants started to roll from the stands: "M.V.P. . . . M.V.P." The Nets went on to wrap up their first title with a 101–88 win. Kidd was certainly at least the MVP of his team, if not the league. "I never thought we would win 50," Kittles said.[6]

Winning the regular season Eastern Conference championship was even more unbelievable. But that is just what the Nets did about a week later. As remarkable an accomplishment as this was, though, the Nets knew that they needed to continue to win in the playoffs to consider their season a success. In the NBA, a team is judged by how far it advances in the playoffs. The Nets had only advanced past the first round once in their previous twenty-five-year playoff history—against Philadelphia in 1984.

For Kidd, it was a personal matter. His playoff experience had been mostly failure—like the Nets, he had only reached the second round once in his NBA career. His teams had lost five of the six series they had played.

The postseason started ominously, with an opening-game loss at home to the Indiana Pacers. But the Nets won three of the next four games—including a double-overtime thriller in Game 5—to advance to the second round. "Right now I'm exhausted," said

Jason Kidd launches a jumpshot during Game 2 of the New Jersey Nets' first-round playoff series against the Indiana Pacers on April 22, 2002.

Kidd after playing 51 of the game's 58 minutes. "I could go for a good night's sleep . . . and then start thinking about Charlotte."[7]

The Nets had been fortunate all season to stay away from key injuries. Their luck finally ended in Game 3 of the playoff series with the Hornets.

It was nearing the end of the second quarter. Kidd was driving for the basket when Charlotte guard David Wesley tipped the ball away from him. The two collided head-on near the foul line and both dropped to the floor. The crowd was eerily silent. Blood began forming a pool near Kidd's head. Trainers rushed onto the court. The Nets' trainer wrapped a towel around Kidd's bloody face and rushed him to the locker room. Wesley was helped to the Hornets' locker room by teammates.

Somehow, Kidd managed to return to the game. He had received about fifteen stitches above his right eye and was wearing a big bandage to protect the injury. He only scored four points the rest of the way as the Nets lost. The Hornets had cut the Nets' series lead to 2–1.

Kidd was hurting, but not enough to keep him out of the playoffs. When Nets trainer Tim Walsh visited Kidd in his hotel room, he saw that the player had shaved his head, a sign he was putting on his game face. "Tim knew I wasn't going to take no for an answer," Kidd said. When the teams took the court for Game 4, there was Kidd out on the court, bruises, bandages, and all.[8]

For Jason Kidd, it was business as usual. He scored 13 of his 24 points in the final eight minutes as the Nets defeated the Hornets, 89–79. Two days later, the Nets clinched the series and by doing so, reached new heights in team history.

But beating the Boston Celtics in the Eastern Conference finals was another matter. After the Nets won the opener with the help of Kidd's forty-fifth career triple-double, they lost two straight to the Celtics. Game 3 of the series was a disaster. The Nets blew a 26-point lead in the third quarter and lost, 94–90. It was the greatest collapse in playoff history. Kidd, who had been given the credit when the Nets were winning, was now taking the blame after this stunning defeat. His leadership came under question.

Kidd was not only feeling bad about the loss. For Kidd, the series had become bitter—and personal. When he was at the foul line late in the game performing his ritual of blowing kisses to his wife, Joumana, the Celtics fans chanted, "Wife beater, wife beater," unmercifully taunting Kidd for his domestic

Kidd puts up a shot over George Lynch of the Charlotte Hornets during the 2002 NBA playoffs.

problems the year before. Even worse, the Kidds' son, T.J., was sitting in the stands at the time.[9]

The Nets simply had to rebound from their most deflating loss of the year, or their season would be over. The Celtics had been a tough team for the Nets all season, winning three of four games. And now the Celtics held a 2–1 lead in this best-of-seven playoff series with the chance to add to their advantage in front of their passionate fans at home. The Celtics had said it was the fans that motivated them in their great comeback win of Game 3.

The Nets knew if they lost the series to Boston, everyone would probably remember their great collapse in Game 3. Their otherwise incredible season would be overshadowed by just another Nets basketball tragedy adding to a long, long list. But the fourth quarter of Game 4 was starting to look suspiciously familiar.

The Nets again took an early lead, and again it started to slip away in the fourth quarter, just as it had in Game 3. Then in the last seven minutes, Kidd stepped in—literally.

After his shot gave the Nets an 82–78 lead, Kidd hustled back on defense. He was planted deep in the lane when Boston's Paul Pierce ran into him. Offensive foul on Pierce. Nets ball.

Jason Kidd's wife, Joumana, and their son, T.J., sit alongside Kidd during a news conference.

Kidd then raced back to the defensive lane again to draw another offensive foul from Pierce. The Nets, leading 86–84 at the time, had the ball back.

With 49.7 seconds left and the Nets leading 92–90, Kidd once more set himself on defense. This time, 255-pound Rodney Rogers ran into him. Another charge call. Another possession for the Nets.

Kidd was known mostly for his offensive talents. Now he was showing off his defense. And he was doing it on the biggest basketball stage of all—the NBA playoffs.

The Nets held on for a 94–92 victory, with

Lucious Harris scoring two clinching free throws at the end. Not surprisingly, it was a nifty pass from the double-teamed Kidd that set up an inside shot for Harris.

The Celtics threw a scare into the Nets in Game 5, rallying from 20 points down to pull within one. Visions of another Game 3 danced in the heads of the Nets fans. But Kidd and Van Horn led a 20–1 blitz as the Nets beat the Celtics 103–92 for a 3–2 series lead. The Nets clinched the series with a 96–88 win in Game 6 behind another triple-double by Kidd. He became the first player in thirty-five years to post three triple-doubles in a playoff series.

"Jason Kidd is off the charts as a player," Celtics coach Jim O'Brien said.[10]

The Nets' storybook season came to an abrupt end with a four-game sweep by the Los Angeles Lakers in the NBA Finals. A disappointment, but the Nets had still come a long way—longer than anyone expected. After winning just 26 games the year before, they had set a team record with 52 victories and played in the NBA Finals for the first time.

How could Kidd and the Nets match the 2001–02 season? How about a repeat as Eastern Conference champions, and a return to the NBA Finals in 2003?

This time the Nets faced the San Antonio Spurs

in a finals series that provided an intriguing story line. Playing in the final year of his Nets contract, Kidd would be a free agent after the season. He still had not made up his mind about returning to New Jersey. In fact, he was thinking about the possibility of joining the Spurs. Kidd loved the idea of playing with Tim Duncan, the Spurs' annual All-Star. Kidd said that playing with the great center would be a dream come true.

But now, on the eve of the Finals, he preferred not to talk about his free-agent plans. "We're at the Finals," he said. "We're trying to win a championship."[11]

Not this time. Kidd and the Nets had an uneven series, taking the Spurs to six games before losing.

Now the Jason Kidd Watch was on. A New Jersey newspaper headlined: "The come back Kidd?" Would he come back to New Jersey or go elsewhere?

Although other teams were interested in Kidd, New Jersey and San Antonio were the only teams he was seriously considering. Kidd knew he would get an incredible contract anywhere he played. But money would not be the deciding factor. More than money, Kidd wanted to win an NBA title.

The Nets were unable to accomplish this goal despite the addition of Dikembe Mutombo in the 2002–03 season. And now, in the summer of 2003,

Nets teammate Jason Collins (35) gives Kidd some defensive help against Tim Duncan of the San Antonio Spurs.

they added Alonzo Mourning while releasing Mutombo.

Deciding on which team to play for was "more difficult than I thought," Kidd said.[12] But he made up his mind once the Nets signed Mourning. He was convinced the Nets were doing everything possible to make their team better.

The headline in a New Jersey newspaper said it all: "Deal Official." Kidd was staying in New Jersey.

The photograph on the sports pages was worth thousands of smiles in New Jersey: Kidd signing his new contract at a news conference—a six-year deal worth $103 million. Standing next to Kidd and watching him sign was his son, T.J.

Kidd was soon off to San Juan, Puerto Rico, to play in an Olympic qualifying tournament, won by the United States. Then it was back to work to prepare for the 2003–04 NBA season.

Nets fans from one end of the state to the other were thrilled. With Kidd in New Jersey, the Nets would again be contenders.

The new season brought many unexpected developments, however. First, there was the sudden retirement of Alonzo Mourning, for health reasons, just a few games into the season. Then, with the team struggling, Head Coach Byron Scott was fired in early 2004 and replaced by assistant Lawrence Frank. Almost immediately after the coaching change, Kidd led the Nets on a franchise-record 14-game winning streak. Despite all the adversity, Kidd appeared poised to lead New Jersey deep into the playoffs once again.

Wherever Kidd has played—high school, college, or pro—his unselfish style has elevated the play of his teammates and made his team better.

"Kids need to watch Jason Kidd and pattern their game after him rather than pattern their games after guys who shoot a lot," said Magic Johnson, the former Lakers great.[13]

Kidd had styled his game after Johnson. Now he was setting an example for a new generation of players.

CHAPTER NOTES

Chapter I. A Most Amazing Game

1. Steve Politi, "Point Guard Preaches Need to Be Aggressive," *Star-Ledger* (Newark, N.J.), May 2, 2002, p. 59.

2. Ibid.

3. Ibid

4. Steve Politi, "The Fantastic Finish—It's Kidd vs. Miller at Crunch Time as Superstars Slug It Out to the End," *Star-Ledger* (Newark, N.J.), May 3, 2002, p. 41.

5. Ibid.

6. Adrian Wojnarowski, "Jason Wasn't About to Let Season End," *Bergen Record* (N.J.), May 3, 2002, p. S1.

7. Fred Kerber, "Nets Work OT for Win—Kidd Trumps Miller in Thriller," *New York Post*, May 3, 2002, p. 116.

8. Ibid.

Chapter 2. Golden Boy

1. Merv Harris, "Hey, Kidd, This Is College and Prep Basketball," *San Francisco Examiner*, March 14, 1991, p. B-5.

2. "Kid(d) stuff—Jason Kidd Let Four Kid Reporters Hang Out with Him. They Had a Blast," *Sports Illustrated for Kids*, February 1, 2000, p. 32.

3. Vlade Olic, "Saved by the Suns," *The Voice*, October 6, 1997, p. 58.
4. Mike Vaccaro, "Kidd's Chance to Show How Great He Can Be," *Star-Ledger* (Newark, N.J.), April 19, 2002, p. 49.
5. Ibid.
6. Scott Ostler, "Kidd Cool on Tourney Chances," *San Francisco Chronicle*, March 14, 1994, p. E1.
7. Richard Witt, "Mavericks' Kidd Forced to Grow Up in a Hurry," *Chicago Tribune*, December 13, 1994, p. 9.
8. Dwight Chapin, "This Guy's a Great Kidd," *San Francisco Examiner*, December 11, 1990, p. C-1.
9. Lonnie White, "St. Joseph Overcomes Fremont," *Los Angeles Times*, March 17, 1991, p. 1.
10. Merv Harris, "Kidd leads St. Joseph to State Crown," *San Francisco Examiner*, March 22, 1992, p. C-1.
11. David Krider, "California Star Kidd Makes Big Name in the Big Games," *USA Today*, April 9, 1992, p. 8C.

Chapter 3. A Golden Bear
1. Frank Blackman, "And a Kidd Shall Lead Them," *San Francisco Examiner*, December 23, 1992, p. B-1.
2. Mark Whicker, "Cal Turns to Kidd Stuff to Recapture Past Glory," *The Orange Country Register* (Calif.), December 25, 1992, p. D1.
3. Bud Withers, "Kidd's Tough Frosh Point Guard the Biggest Thing to Hit California Since the Gold Rush," *Seattle Post-Intelligencer*, January 28, 1993, p. D1.
4. Ray Ratto, "The Pot's Still Bubbling at Cal," *San Francisco Examiner*, February 18, 1993, p. B-1.

5. Tony Cooper, " 'New' Bears Run Past Stanford," *San Francisco Chronicle*, February 15, 1993, p. C1.

6. Toni Ginnetti, "Kid's Late Shot Lifts Cal past LSU," *Chicago Sun-Times*, March 19, 1993, p. 120.

7. Ibid.

8. Ibid.

9. Skip Myslenski, "The King (Duke) Is Dead," *Chicago Tribune*, March 21, 1993, p. 1.

10. Elton Alexander, "California Knocks Off Duke, 82-77," *The Cleveland Plain Dealer*, March 21, 1993, p. 1D.

Chapter 4. The Next Level

1. Scott Ostler, "Kidd's Performance Was All We Needed to See," *The San Francisco Chronicle*, March 4, 1994, p. B1.

2. Ibid.

3. Associated Press report, "Mavs, Kidd Agree to $60 Million Pact," *Tulsa World*, September 4, 1994, p. S12.

4. Kerry Eggers, "Kidd Is Bringing Mavericks' Running Game to His Level," *Portland Oregonian*, October 25, 1994, p. D2.

5. Ibid.

6. Randy Galloway, "Mavericks Not Only Win, They Prove Entertaining," *The Dallas Morning News*, December 6, 1994, p. 4B.

7. Frank Hughes, "No Kidding—Rookie Transforms Sad-Sack Mavs," *The Washington Times*, December 9, 1994, p. B1.

8. Glenn Nelson, "Star Search—Mavericks' Kidd Gets Rave Reviews, but Maybe Not Award," *The Seattle Times*, April 13, 1995.

Chapter 5. All-Star Kidd

1. Associated Press report, "Kidd Puts on a Show for All-Star Fans," *The Columbian*, February 12, 1996, p. B4.
2. Ibid.
3. Jerry Briggs, "No Kidd-ing: Jason Silences Critics," *San Antonio Express-News*, February 12, 1996.
4. Brad Townsend, "The Call of Fame," *The Dallas Morning News*, February 12, 1996, p. 1B.
5. Mark Bechtel, "Midwest Scouting Reports—5 Dallas Mavericks," *Sports Illustrated*, November 1, 1996, p. 136.
6. Ibid.
7. Johnette Howard, "The Ball's in His Hands," *Sports Illustrated*, November 11, 1996, p. 94.
8. Jaime Aron (The Associated Press), "New Suns Guard Kidd Is Hoping to Find Himself in Phoenix," *The Salt Lake Tribune,* December 28, 1996, p. E7.
9. Dave Caldwell, "Colossal Collapse," *The Dallas Morning News,* March 3, 1997, p. 1B.
10. Vicki Michaelis, "You're Kidding? Suns Sing Praises of Point Guard Acquired in Deal with Mavericks," *Denver Post*, April 4, 1997, p. C-12.
11. Andrea N. Whittaker, "Get the Point!", *Sports Illustrated For Kids*, June 1, 1999, p. 64.

Chapter 6. Bumpy Season, Breakout Game

1. "Suns Lose Kidd for Season," *Seattle Times*, March 23, 2000, p. D10.
2. Bob Baum, "Despite Awful Finale, Suns Consider Season a Success," *The Canadian Press* from Associated Press report, May 17, 2000.
3. Bob Baum, "Suns Finish Off Spurs with an 89–78 Victory," *Portland Oregonian*, May 3, 2000, p. E3.

4. David Leon Moore, "Kidd's Play is Suns' Bright Spot," *USA Today*, May 3, 2000, p. 13C.

5. Steve Dilbeck, "Suns Face Adversity," *Los Angeles Daily News*, May 14, 2000, p. S5.

6. "Stayin' Alive," *The Grand Rapids Press*, May 15, 2000, p. D3.

7. Kevin Ding, "Kidd Energizes the Suns," *The Orange County Register*, May 15, 2000, p. D6.

Chapter 7. Golden

1. John Crumpacker, "Jason's Like a Kidd in a Candy Store," *San Francisco Examiner,* September 3, 2000, p. E-1.

2. Ibid.

3. Geoffrey C. Arnold, " 'Disrespect' Fires Up U.S. Basketball Team," *Portland Oregonian*, September 15, 2000, p. D5.

4. Ibid.

5. Robyn Norwood, "It's Almost a Nightmare for U.S. Men's Basketball," *Los Angeles Times*, September 30, 2000, p. U-1.

6. Gwen Knapp, "Dreamers limp to gold," *San Francisco Examiner*, October 1, 2000, p. C-1.

7. Phil Taylor, David Sabino, "Breathtaking," *Sports Illustrated*, December 4, 2000, pp. 63–64.

8. Bob Baum, "Point Guard Jason Kidd Faces Domestic Abuse Charge for Hitting His Wife," *Canadian Press* from Associated Press report, January 19, 2001.

9. Bob Baum, "Jason Kidd Comes Back from Off Court Woes to Play Better Than Ever," *Canadian Press* from Associated Press report, March 21, 2001.

10. David Steele, "Kidd Faces Questions About Ugliest Incident," *The San Francisco Chronicle*, February 13, 2001, p. E1.

11. Dan McGrath, "This Kidd Can Really Play," *Chicago Tribune*, April 26, 2001, p. 1.

Chapter 8. Jason to the Rescue

1. S.L. Price, "A Clean Start," *Sports Illustrated*, January 28, 2002, p. 64.
2. Scott Soshnick, "Boring Jason Makes a Point," *The Seattle Times*, December 6, 2001, p. D7.
3. Price, p. 63.
4. Liz Robbins, "Kidd Upgrades His Game as Nets Surge Past the Spurs," *The New York Times*, January 23, 2002, p. 1.
5. Liz Robbins, "Nets Are Redefining Meaning of Success," *The New York Times*, January 24, 2002, p. 8.
6. Liz Robbins, "Nets Win Their Division," *The New York Times*, April 10, 2002, p. 1.
7. Steve Politi, "The Fantastic Finish—It's Kidd vs. Miller at Crunch Time as Superstars Slug It Out to the End," *The Star-Ledger* (Newark, N.J.), May 3, 2002, p. 41.
8. Barbara Barker, "Puffy Eye, Tight Focus," *New York Newsday*, May 13, 2002, p. A46.
9. Shaun Powell, "Bouncing Back in Style," *New York Newsday*, May 28, 2002, p. A51.
10. Diane Pucin, "Kidd's Numbers Don't Lie as Nets Finish off Celtics," *Los Angeles Times*, June 1, 2002, p. D-11.
11. Bob Considine, "Questions About Kidd's Future Continue," *Home News Tribune* (New Brunswick, N.J.), May 28, 2003, p. D7.
12. Bob Considine, "Deal Official," *Home News Tribune* (New Brunswick, N.J.), July 25, 2003, p. C1.
13. Tim Kawakami, "Kidd Needs Running Mate If He's Ever to Win a Ring," *San Jose Mercury News*, June 12, 2002, p. 1.

CAREER STATISTICS

COLLEGE

Team	Year	G	FG%	REB	AST	PTS	AVG
California	1992–93	29	.463	142	222	378	13.0
California	1992–93	30	.472	207	272	500	16.7
TOTALS		59	.468	349	494	878	14.9

G—Games   **REB**—Rebounds   **PTS**—Points
FG%—Field   **AST**—Assists   **AVG**—Average
Goal percentage

NBA

Team	Year	G	FG%	REB	AST	STL	BLK	PTS	AVG
Dallas	1994–95	79	.385	430	607	151	24	922	11.7
Dallas	1995–96	81	.381	553	783	175	26	1,348	16.6
Dallas	1996–97	22	.369	90	200	45	8	217	9.9
Phoenix	1996–97	33	.423	159	296	79	12	382	11.6
Phoenix	1997–98	82	.416	510	745	162	26	954	11.6
Phoenix	1998–99	50	.444	339	539	114	19	846	16.9
Phoenix	1999–00	67	.409	483	678	134	28	959	14.3
Phoenix	2000–01	77	.411	494	753	166	23	1,299	16.9
New Jersey	2001–02	82	.391	595	808	175	20	1,208	14.7
New Jersey	2002–03	80	.414	504	711	179	25	1,495	18.7
New Jersey	2003-04	67	.384	428	618	122	14	1,036	15.5
TOTALS		720	.402	4,585	6,738	1,502	225	10,666	14.8

G—Games **REB**—Rebounds **BLK**—Blocks
FG%—Field **AST**—Assists **PTS**—Points
Goal percentage **STL**—Steals **AVG**—Average

WHERE TO WRITE

Mr. Jason Kidd
c/o The New Jersey Nets
Continental Airlines Arena
Meadowlands Sports Complex
50 Route 120
East Rutherford, NJ 07073

INTERNET ADDRESSES

Jason Kidd Bio

http://www.nba.com/playerfile/jason_kidd/index.
  html?nav=page

NBA.com

http://www.nba.com

INDEX

3/12 ⑮
1/14 ⑰